FOOD DIARY
&
SYMPTOM LOG

NAME:

PHONE NUMBER:

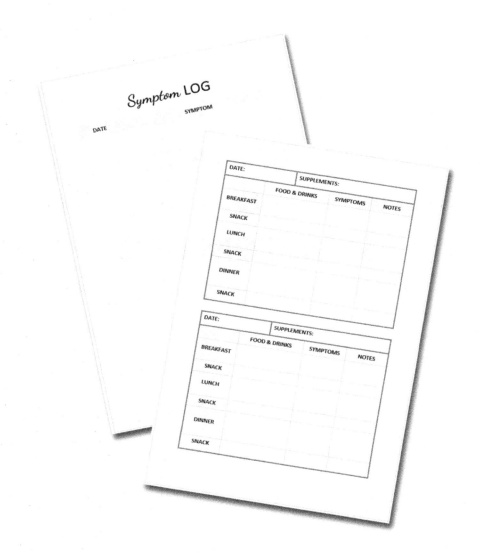

Tealous Books

Available from Amazon.com and other online stores.

Symptom LOG

DATE	SYMPTOM

Symptom LOG

DATE	SYMPTOM

Symptom LOG

DATE	SYMPTOM	

Symptom LOG

DATE	SYMPTOM

Symptom LOG

DATE	SYMPTOM

Symptom LOG

DATE	SYMPTOM

Symptom LOG

DATE	SYMPTOM

Symptom LOG

DATE	SYMPTOM

DAILY FOOD

Diary

DATE:		SUPPLEMENTS:	
	FOOD & DRINKS	SYMPTOMS	NOTES
BREAKFAST			
SNACK			
LUNCH			
SNACK			
DINNER			
SNACK			

DATE:		SUPPLEMENTS:	
	FOOD & DRINKS	SYMPTOMS	NOTES
BREAKFAST			
SNACK			
LUNCH			
SNACK			
DINNER			
SNACK			

DATE:	SUPPLEMENTS:		
	FOOD & DRINKS	**SYMPTOMS**	**NOTES**
BREAKFAST			
SNACK			
LUNCH			
SNACK			
DINNER			
SNACK			

DATE:	SUPPLEMENTS:		
	FOOD & DRINKS	**SYMPTOMS**	**NOTES**
BREAKFAST			
SNACK			
LUNCH			
SNACK			
DINNER			
SNACK			

DATE:	SUPPLEMENTS:		
	FOOD & DRINKS	SYMPTOMS	NOTES
BREAKFAST			
SNACK			
LUNCH			
SNACK			
DINNER			
SNACK			

DATE:	SUPPLEMENTS:		
	FOOD & DRINKS	SYMPTOMS	NOTES
BREAKFAST			
SNACK			
LUNCH			
SNACK			
DINNER			
SNACK			

DATE:	SUPPLEMENTS:		
	FOOD & DRINKS	SYMPTOMS	NOTES
BREAKFAST			
SNACK			
LUNCH			
SNACK			
DINNER			
SNACK			

DATE:	SUPPLEMENTS:		
	FOOD & DRINKS	SYMPTOMS	NOTES
BREAKFAST			
SNACK			
LUNCH			
SNACK			
DINNER			
SNACK			

DATE:	SUPPLEMENTS:		
	FOOD & DRINKS	**SYMPTOMS**	**NOTES**
BREAKFAST			
SNACK			
LUNCH			
SNACK			
DINNER			
SNACK			

DATE:	SUPPLEMENTS:		
	FOOD & DRINKS	**SYMPTOMS**	**NOTES**
BREAKFAST			
SNACK			
LUNCH			
SNACK			
DINNER			
SNACK			

DATE:	SUPPLEMENTS:		
	FOOD & DRINKS	SYMPTOMS	NOTES
BREAKFAST			
SNACK			
LUNCH			
SNACK			
DINNER			
SNACK			

DATE:	SUPPLEMENTS:		
	FOOD & DRINKS	SYMPTOMS	NOTES
BREAKFAST			
SNACK			
LUNCH			
SNACK			
DINNER			
SNACK			

DATE:	SUPPLEMENTS:		
	FOOD & DRINKS	SYMPTOMS	NOTES
BREAKFAST			
SNACK			
LUNCH			
SNACK			
DINNER			
SNACK			

DATE:	SUPPLEMENTS:		
	FOOD & DRINKS	SYMPTOMS	NOTES
BREAKFAST			
SNACK			
LUNCH			
SNACK			
DINNER			
SNACK			

DATE:	SUPPLEMENTS:		
	FOOD & DRINKS	**SYMPTOMS**	**NOTES**
BREAKFAST			
SNACK			
LUNCH			
SNACK			
DINNER			
SNACK			

DATE:	SUPPLEMENTS:		
	FOOD & DRINKS	**SYMPTOMS**	**NOTES**
BREAKFAST			
SNACK			
LUNCH			
SNACK			
DINNER			
SNACK			

DATE:	SUPPLEMENTS:		
	FOOD & DRINKS	**SYMPTOMS**	**NOTES**
BREAKFAST			
SNACK			
LUNCH			
SNACK			
DINNER			
SNACK			

DATE:	SUPPLEMENTS:		
	FOOD & DRINKS	**SYMPTOMS**	**NOTES**
BREAKFAST			
SNACK			
LUNCH			
SNACK			
DINNER			
SNACK			

DATE:	SUPPLEMENTS:		
	FOOD & DRINKS	**SYMPTOMS**	**NOTES**
BREAKFAST			
SNACK			
LUNCH			
SNACK			
DINNER			
SNACK			

DATE:	SUPPLEMENTS:		
	FOOD & DRINKS	**SYMPTOMS**	**NOTES**
BREAKFAST			
SNACK			
LUNCH			
SNACK			
DINNER			
SNACK			

DATE:	SUPPLEMENTS:		
	FOOD & DRINKS	SYMPTOMS	NOTES
BREAKFAST			
SNACK			
LUNCH			
SNACK			
DINNER			
SNACK			

DATE:	SUPPLEMENTS:		
	FOOD & DRINKS	SYMPTOMS	NOTES
BREAKFAST			
SNACK			
LUNCH			
SNACK			
DINNER			
SNACK			

DATE:	SUPPLEMENTS:		
	FOOD & DRINKS	**SYMPTOMS**	**NOTES**
BREAKFAST			
SNACK			
LUNCH			
SNACK			
DINNER			
SNACK			

DATE:	SUPPLEMENTS:		
	FOOD & DRINKS	**SYMPTOMS**	**NOTES**
BREAKFAST			
SNACK			
LUNCH			
SNACK			
DINNER			
SNACK			

DATE:	SUPPLEMENTS:		
	FOOD & DRINKS	SYMPTOMS	NOTES
BREAKFAST			
SNACK			
LUNCH			
SNACK			
DINNER			
SNACK			

DATE:	SUPPLEMENTS:		
	FOOD & DRINKS	SYMPTOMS	NOTES
BREAKFAST			
SNACK			
LUNCH			
SNACK			
DINNER			
SNACK			

DATE:	SUPPLEMENTS:		
	FOOD & DRINKS	**SYMPTOMS**	**NOTES**
BREAKFAST			
SNACK			
LUNCH			
SNACK			
DINNER			
SNACK			

DATE:	SUPPLEMENTS:		
	FOOD & DRINKS	**SYMPTOMS**	**NOTES**
BREAKFAST			
SNACK			
LUNCH			
SNACK			
DINNER			
SNACK			

DATE:	SUPPLEMENTS:		
	FOOD & DRINKS	**SYMPTOMS**	**NOTES**
BREAKFAST			
SNACK			
LUNCH			
SNACK			
DINNER			
SNACK			

DATE:	SUPPLEMENTS:		
	FOOD & DRINKS	**SYMPTOMS**	**NOTES**
BREAKFAST			
SNACK			
LUNCH			
SNACK			
DINNER			
SNACK			

DATE:	SUPPLEMENTS:		
	FOOD & DRINKS	**SYMPTOMS**	**NOTES**
BREAKFAST			
SNACK			
LUNCH			
SNACK			
DINNER			
SNACK			

DATE:	SUPPLEMENTS:		
	FOOD & DRINKS	**SYMPTOMS**	**NOTES**
BREAKFAST			
SNACK			
LUNCH			
SNACK			
DINNER			
SNACK			

DATE:	SUPPLEMENTS:		
	FOOD & DRINKS	**SYMPTOMS**	**NOTES**
BREAKFAST			
SNACK			
LUNCH			
SNACK			
DINNER			
SNACK			

DATE:	SUPPLEMENTS:		
	FOOD & DRINKS	**SYMPTOMS**	**NOTES**
BREAKFAST			
SNACK			
LUNCH			
SNACK			
DINNER			
SNACK			

DATE:	SUPPLEMENTS:		
	FOOD & DRINKS	**SYMPTOMS**	**NOTES**
BREAKFAST			
SNACK			
LUNCH			
SNACK			
DINNER			
SNACK			

DATE:	SUPPLEMENTS:		
	FOOD & DRINKS	**SYMPTOMS**	**NOTES**
BREAKFAST			
SNACK			
LUNCH			
SNACK			
DINNER			
SNACK			

DATE:	SUPPLEMENTS:		
	FOOD & DRINKS	**SYMPTOMS**	**NOTES**
BREAKFAST			
SNACK			
LUNCH			
SNACK			
DINNER			
SNACK			

DATE:	SUPPLEMENTS:		
	FOOD & DRINKS	**SYMPTOMS**	**NOTES**
BREAKFAST			
SNACK			
LUNCH			
SNACK			
DINNER			
SNACK			

DATE:	SUPPLEMENTS:		
	FOOD & DRINKS	**SYMPTOMS**	**NOTES**
BREAKFAST			
SNACK			
LUNCH			
SNACK			
DINNER			
SNACK			

DATE:	SUPPLEMENTS:		
	FOOD & DRINKS	**SYMPTOMS**	**NOTES**
BREAKFAST			
SNACK			
LUNCH			
SNACK			
DINNER			
SNACK			

DATE:	SUPPLEMENTS:		
	FOOD & DRINKS	**SYMPTOMS**	**NOTES**
BREAKFAST			
SNACK			
LUNCH			
SNACK			
DINNER			
SNACK			

DATE:	SUPPLEMENTS:		
	FOOD & DRINKS	**SYMPTOMS**	**NOTES**
BREAKFAST			
SNACK			
LUNCH			
SNACK			
DINNER			
SNACK			

DATE:	SUPPLEMENTS:		
	FOOD & DRINKS	**SYMPTOMS**	**NOTES**
BREAKFAST			
SNACK			
LUNCH			
SNACK			
DINNER			
SNACK			

DATE:	SUPPLEMENTS:		
	FOOD & DRINKS	**SYMPTOMS**	**NOTES**
BREAKFAST			
SNACK			
LUNCH			
SNACK			
DINNER			
SNACK			

DATE:		SUPPLEMENTS:		
	FOOD & DRINKS	**SYMPTOMS**	**NOTES**	
BREAKFAST				
SNACK				
LUNCH				
SNACK				
DINNER				
SNACK				

DATE:		SUPPLEMENTS:		
	FOOD & DRINKS	**SYMPTOMS**	**NOTES**	
BREAKFAST				
SNACK				
LUNCH				
SNACK				
DINNER				
SNACK				

DATE:	SUPPLEMENTS:		
	FOOD & DRINKS	**SYMPTOMS**	**NOTES**
BREAKFAST			
SNACK			
LUNCH			
SNACK			
DINNER			
SNACK			

DATE:	SUPPLEMENTS:		
	FOOD & DRINKS	**SYMPTOMS**	**NOTES**
BREAKFAST			
SNACK			
LUNCH			
SNACK			
DINNER			
SNACK			

DATE:	SUPPLEMENTS:		
	FOOD & DRINKS	**SYMPTOMS**	**NOTES**
BREAKFAST			
SNACK			
LUNCH			
SNACK			
DINNER			
SNACK			

DATE:	SUPPLEMENTS:		
	FOOD & DRINKS	**SYMPTOMS**	**NOTES**
BREAKFAST			
SNACK			
LUNCH			
SNACK			
DINNER			
SNACK			

DATE:	SUPPLEMENTS:		
	FOOD & DRINKS	**SYMPTOMS**	**NOTES**
BREAKFAST			
SNACK			
LUNCH			
SNACK			
DINNER			
SNACK			

DATE:	SUPPLEMENTS:		
	FOOD & DRINKS	**SYMPTOMS**	**NOTES**
BREAKFAST			
SNACK			
LUNCH			
SNACK			
DINNER			
SNACK			

DATE:	SUPPLEMENTS:		
	FOOD & DRINKS	**SYMPTOMS**	**NOTES**
BREAKFAST			
SNACK			
LUNCH			
SNACK			
DINNER			
SNACK			

DATE:	SUPPLEMENTS:		
	FOOD & DRINKS	**SYMPTOMS**	**NOTES**
BREAKFAST			
SNACK			
LUNCH			
SNACK			
DINNER			
SNACK			

DATE:	SUPPLEMENTS:		
	FOOD & DRINKS	SYMPTOMS	NOTES
BREAKFAST			
SNACK			
LUNCH			
SNACK			
DINNER			
SNACK			

DATE:	SUPPLEMENTS:		
	FOOD & DRINKS	SYMPTOMS	NOTES
BREAKFAST			
SNACK			
LUNCH			
SNACK			
DINNER			
SNACK			

DATE:	SUPPLEMENTS:		
	FOOD & DRINKS	**SYMPTOMS**	**NOTES**
BREAKFAST			
SNACK			
LUNCH			
SNACK			
DINNER			
SNACK			

DATE:	SUPPLEMENTS:		
	FOOD & DRINKS	**SYMPTOMS**	**NOTES**
BREAKFAST			
SNACK			
LUNCH			
SNACK			
DINNER			
SNACK			

DATE:		SUPPLEMENTS:	
	FOOD & DRINKS	**SYMPTOMS**	**NOTES**
BREAKFAST			
SNACK			
LUNCH			
SNACK			
DINNER			
SNACK			

DATE:		SUPPLEMENTS:	
	FOOD & DRINKS	**SYMPTOMS**	**NOTES**
BREAKFAST			
SNACK			
LUNCH			
SNACK			
DINNER			
SNACK			

DATE:	SUPPLEMENTS:		
	FOOD & DRINKS	SYMPTOMS	NOTES
BREAKFAST			
SNACK			
LUNCH			
SNACK			
DINNER			
SNACK			

DATE:	SUPPLEMENTS:		
	FOOD & DRINKS	SYMPTOMS	NOTES
BREAKFAST			
SNACK			
LUNCH			
SNACK			
DINNER			
SNACK			

DATE:	SUPPLEMENTS:		
	FOOD & DRINKS	**SYMPTOMS**	**NOTES**
BREAKFAST			
SNACK			
LUNCH			
SNACK			
DINNER			
SNACK			

DATE:	SUPPLEMENTS:		
	FOOD & DRINKS	**SYMPTOMS**	**NOTES**
BREAKFAST			
SNACK			
LUNCH			
SNACK			
DINNER			
SNACK			

DATE:	SUPPLEMENTS:		
	FOOD & DRINKS	SYMPTOMS	NOTES
BREAKFAST			
SNACK			
LUNCH			
SNACK			
DINNER			
SNACK			

DATE:	SUPPLEMENTS:		
	FOOD & DRINKS	SYMPTOMS	NOTES
BREAKFAST			
SNACK			
LUNCH			
SNACK			
DINNER			
SNACK			

DATE:	SUPPLEMENTS:		
	FOOD & DRINKS	**SYMPTOMS**	**NOTES**
BREAKFAST			
SNACK			
LUNCH			
SNACK			
DINNER			
SNACK			

DATE:	SUPPLEMENTS:		
	FOOD & DRINKS	**SYMPTOMS**	**NOTES**
BREAKFAST			
SNACK			
LUNCH			
SNACK			
DINNER			
SNACK			

DATE:	SUPPLEMENTS:		
	FOOD & DRINKS	SYMPTOMS	NOTES
BREAKFAST			
SNACK			
LUNCH			
SNACK			
DINNER			
SNACK			

DATE:	SUPPLEMENTS:		
	FOOD & DRINKS	SYMPTOMS	NOTES
BREAKFAST			
SNACK			
LUNCH			
SNACK			
DINNER			
SNACK			

DATE:	SUPPLEMENTS:		
	FOOD & DRINKS	SYMPTOMS	NOTES
BREAKFAST			
SNACK			
LUNCH			
SNACK			
DINNER			
SNACK			

DATE:	SUPPLEMENTS:		
	FOOD & DRINKS	SYMPTOMS	NOTES
BREAKFAST			
SNACK			
LUNCH			
SNACK			
DINNER			
SNACK			

DATE:	SUPPLEMENTS:		
	FOOD & DRINKS	**SYMPTOMS**	**NOTES**
BREAKFAST			
SNACK			
LUNCH			
SNACK			
DINNER			
SNACK			

DATE:	SUPPLEMENTS:		
	FOOD & DRINKS	**SYMPTOMS**	**NOTES**
BREAKFAST			
SNACK			
LUNCH			
SNACK			
DINNER			
SNACK			

DATE:	SUPPLEMENTS:		
	FOOD & DRINKS	**SYMPTOMS**	**NOTES**
BREAKFAST			
SNACK			
LUNCH			
SNACK			
DINNER			
SNACK			

DATE:	SUPPLEMENTS:		
	FOOD & DRINKS	**SYMPTOMS**	**NOTES**
BREAKFAST			
SNACK			
LUNCH			
SNACK			
DINNER			
SNACK			

DATE:	SUPPLEMENTS:		
	FOOD & DRINKS	**SYMPTOMS**	**NOTES**
BREAKFAST			
SNACK			
LUNCH			
SNACK			
DINNER			
SNACK			

DATE:	SUPPLEMENTS:		
	FOOD & DRINKS	**SYMPTOMS**	**NOTES**
BREAKFAST			
SNACK			
LUNCH			
SNACK			
DINNER			
SNACK			

DATE:	SUPPLEMENTS:		
	FOOD & DRINKS	**SYMPTOMS**	**NOTES**
BREAKFAST			
SNACK			
LUNCH			
SNACK			
DINNER			
SNACK			

DATE:	SUPPLEMENTS:		
	FOOD & DRINKS	**SYMPTOMS**	**NOTES**
BREAKFAST			
SNACK			
LUNCH			
SNACK			
DINNER			
SNACK			

DATE:	SUPPLEMENTS:		
	FOOD & DRINKS	**SYMPTOMS**	**NOTES**
BREAKFAST			
SNACK			
LUNCH			
SNACK			
DINNER			
SNACK			

DATE:	SUPPLEMENTS:		
	FOOD & DRINKS	**SYMPTOMS**	**NOTES**
BREAKFAST			
SNACK			
LUNCH			
SNACK			
DINNER			
SNACK			

DATE:	SUPPLEMENTS:		
	FOOD & DRINKS	**SYMPTOMS**	**NOTES**
BREAKFAST			
SNACK			
LUNCH			
SNACK			
DINNER			
SNACK			

DATE:	SUPPLEMENTS:		
	FOOD & DRINKS	**SYMPTOMS**	**NOTES**
BREAKFAST			
SNACK			
LUNCH			
SNACK			
DINNER			
SNACK			

DATE:	SUPPLEMENTS:		
	FOOD & DRINKS	SYMPTOMS	NOTES
BREAKFAST			
SNACK			
LUNCH			
SNACK			
DINNER			
SNACK			

DATE:	SUPPLEMENTS:		
	FOOD & DRINKS	SYMPTOMS	NOTES
BREAKFAST			
SNACK			
LUNCH			
SNACK			
DINNER			
SNACK			

DATE:	SUPPLEMENTS:		
	FOOD & DRINKS	**SYMPTOMS**	**NOTES**
BREAKFAST			
SNACK			
LUNCH			
SNACK			
DINNER			
SNACK			

DATE:	SUPPLEMENTS:		
	FOOD & DRINKS	**SYMPTOMS**	**NOTES**
BREAKFAST			
SNACK			
LUNCH			
SNACK			
DINNER			
SNACK			

DATE:	SUPPLEMENTS:		
	FOOD & DRINKS	**SYMPTOMS**	**NOTES**
BREAKFAST			
SNACK			
LUNCH			
SNACK			
DINNER			
SNACK			

DATE:	SUPPLEMENTS:		
	FOOD & DRINKS	**SYMPTOMS**	**NOTES**
BREAKFAST			
SNACK			
LUNCH			
SNACK			
DINNER			
SNACK			

DATE:	SUPPLEMENTS:		
	FOOD & DRINKS	**SYMPTOMS**	**NOTES**
BREAKFAST			
SNACK			
LUNCH			
SNACK			
DINNER			
SNACK			

DATE:	SUPPLEMENTS:		
	FOOD & DRINKS	**SYMPTOMS**	**NOTES**
BREAKFAST			
SNACK			
LUNCH			
SNACK			
DINNER			
SNACK			

DATE:	SUPPLEMENTS:		
	FOOD & DRINKS	SYMPTOMS	NOTES
BREAKFAST			
SNACK			
LUNCH			
SNACK			
DINNER			
SNACK			

DATE:	SUPPLEMENTS:		
	FOOD & DRINKS	SYMPTOMS	NOTES
BREAKFAST			
SNACK			
LUNCH			
SNACK			
DINNER			
SNACK			

DATE:	SUPPLEMENTS:		
	FOOD & DRINKS	SYMPTOMS	NOTES
BREAKFAST			
SNACK			
LUNCH			
SNACK			
DINNER			
SNACK			

DATE:	SUPPLEMENTS:		
	FOOD & DRINKS	SYMPTOMS	NOTES
BREAKFAST			
SNACK			
LUNCH			
SNACK			
DINNER			
SNACK			

DATE:	SUPPLEMENTS:		
	FOOD & DRINKS	SYMPTOMS	NOTES
BREAKFAST			
SNACK			
LUNCH			
SNACK			
DINNER			
SNACK			

DATE:	SUPPLEMENTS:		
	FOOD & DRINKS	SYMPTOMS	NOTES
BREAKFAST			
SNACK			
LUNCH			
SNACK			
DINNER			
SNACK			

DATE:	SUPPLEMENTS:		
	FOOD & DRINKS	SYMPTOMS	NOTES
BREAKFAST			
SNACK			
LUNCH			
SNACK			
DINNER			
SNACK			

DATE:	SUPPLEMENTS:		
	FOOD & DRINKS	SYMPTOMS	NOTES
BREAKFAST			
SNACK			
LUNCH			
SNACK			
DINNER			
SNACK			

DATE:		SUPPLEMENTS:	
	FOOD & DRINKS	**SYMPTOMS**	**NOTES**
BREAKFAST			
SNACK			
LUNCH			
SNACK			
DINNER			
SNACK			

DATE:		SUPPLEMENTS:	
	FOOD & DRINKS	**SYMPTOMS**	**NOTES**
BREAKFAST			
SNACK			
LUNCH			
SNACK			
DINNER			
SNACK			

DATE:	SUPPLEMENTS:		
	FOOD & DRINKS	**SYMPTOMS**	**NOTES**
BREAKFAST			
SNACK			
LUNCH			
SNACK			
DINNER			
SNACK			

DATE:	SUPPLEMENTS:		
	FOOD & DRINKS	**SYMPTOMS**	**NOTES**
BREAKFAST			
SNACK			
LUNCH			
SNACK			
DINNER			
SNACK			

DATE:	SUPPLEMENTS:		
	FOOD & DRINKS	**SYMPTOMS**	**NOTES**
BREAKFAST			
SNACK			
LUNCH			
SNACK			
DINNER			
SNACK			

DATE:	SUPPLEMENTS:		
	FOOD & DRINKS	**SYMPTOMS**	**NOTES**
BREAKFAST			
SNACK			
LUNCH			
SNACK			
DINNER			
SNACK			

DATE:	SUPPLEMENTS:		
	FOOD & DRINKS	**SYMPTOMS**	**NOTES**
BREAKFAST			
SNACK			
LUNCH			
SNACK			
DINNER			
SNACK			

DATE:	SUPPLEMENTS:		
	FOOD & DRINKS	**SYMPTOMS**	**NOTES**
BREAKFAST			
SNACK			
LUNCH			
SNACK			
DINNER			
SNACK			

DATE:	SUPPLEMENTS:		
	FOOD & DRINKS	SYMPTOMS	NOTES
BREAKFAST			
SNACK			
LUNCH			
SNACK			
DINNER			
SNACK			

DATE:	SUPPLEMENTS:		
	FOOD & DRINKS	SYMPTOMS	NOTES
BREAKFAST			
SNACK			
LUNCH			
SNACK			
DINNER			
SNACK			

DATE:	SUPPLEMENTS:		
	FOOD & DRINKS	**SYMPTOMS**	**NOTES**
BREAKFAST			
SNACK			
LUNCH			
SNACK			
DINNER			
SNACK			

DATE:	SUPPLEMENTS:		
	FOOD & DRINKS	**SYMPTOMS**	**NOTES**
BREAKFAST			
SNACK			
LUNCH			
SNACK			
DINNER			
SNACK			

DATE:	SUPPLEMENTS:		
	FOOD & DRINKS	**SYMPTOMS**	**NOTES**
BREAKFAST			
SNACK			
LUNCH			
SNACK			
DINNER			
SNACK			

DATE:	SUPPLEMENTS:		
	FOOD & DRINKS	**SYMPTOMS**	**NOTES**
BREAKFAST			
SNACK			
LUNCH			
SNACK			
DINNER			
SNACK			

DATE:	SUPPLEMENTS:		
	FOOD & DRINKS	**SYMPTOMS**	**NOTES**
BREAKFAST			
SNACK			
LUNCH			
SNACK			
DINNER			
SNACK			

DATE:	SUPPLEMENTS:		
	FOOD & DRINKS	**SYMPTOMS**	**NOTES**
BREAKFAST			
SNACK			
LUNCH			
SNACK			
DINNER			
SNACK			

DATE:	SUPPLEMENTS:		
	FOOD & DRINKS	SYMPTOMS	NOTES
BREAKFAST			
SNACK			
LUNCH			
SNACK			
DINNER			
SNACK			

DATE:	SUPPLEMENTS:		
	FOOD & DRINKS	SYMPTOMS	NOTES
BREAKFAST			
SNACK			
LUNCH			
SNACK			
DINNER			
SNACK			

DATE:	SUPPLEMENTS:		
	FOOD & DRINKS	**SYMPTOMS**	**NOTES**
BREAKFAST			
SNACK			
LUNCH			
SNACK			
DINNER			
SNACK			

DATE:	SUPPLEMENTS:		
	FOOD & DRINKS	**SYMPTOMS**	**NOTES**
BREAKFAST			
SNACK			
LUNCH			
SNACK			
DINNER			
SNACK			

DATE:	SUPPLEMENTS:		
	FOOD & DRINKS	SYMPTOMS	NOTES
BREAKFAST			
SNACK			
LUNCH			
SNACK			
DINNER			
SNACK			

DATE:	SUPPLEMENTS:		
	FOOD & DRINKS	SYMPTOMS	NOTES
BREAKFAST			
SNACK			
LUNCH			
SNACK			
DINNER			
SNACK			

DATE:		SUPPLEMENTS:	
	FOOD & DRINKS	SYMPTOMS	NOTES
BREAKFAST			
SNACK			
LUNCH			
SNACK			
DINNER			
SNACK			

DATE:		SUPPLEMENTS:	
	FOOD & DRINKS	SYMPTOMS	NOTES
BREAKFAST			
SNACK			
LUNCH			
SNACK			
DINNER			
SNACK			

DATE:	SUPPLEMENTS:		
	FOOD & DRINKS	SYMPTOMS	NOTES
BREAKFAST			
SNACK			
LUNCH			
SNACK			
DINNER			
SNACK			

DATE:	SUPPLEMENTS:		
	FOOD & DRINKS	SYMPTOMS	NOTES
BREAKFAST			
SNACK			
LUNCH			
SNACK			
DINNER			
SNACK			

DATE:		SUPPLEMENTS:	
	FOOD & DRINKS	**SYMPTOMS**	**NOTES**
BREAKFAST			
SNACK			
LUNCH			
SNACK			
DINNER			
SNACK			

DATE:		SUPPLEMENTS:	
	FOOD & DRINKS	**SYMPTOMS**	**NOTES**
BREAKFAST			
SNACK			
LUNCH			
SNACK			
DINNER			
SNACK			

DATE:	SUPPLEMENTS:		
	FOOD & DRINKS	SYMPTOMS	NOTES
BREAKFAST			
SNACK			
LUNCH			
SNACK			
DINNER			
SNACK			

DATE:	SUPPLEMENTS:		
	FOOD & DRINKS	SYMPTOMS	NOTES
BREAKFAST			
SNACK			
LUNCH			
SNACK			
DINNER			
SNACK			

DATE:	SUPPLEMENTS:		
	FOOD & DRINKS	**SYMPTOMS**	**NOTES**
BREAKFAST			
SNACK			
LUNCH			
SNACK			
DINNER			
SNACK			

DATE:	SUPPLEMENTS:		
	FOOD & DRINKS	**SYMPTOMS**	**NOTES**
BREAKFAST			
SNACK			
LUNCH			
SNACK			
DINNER			
SNACK			

DATE:	SUPPLEMENTS:		
	FOOD & DRINKS	**SYMPTOMS**	**NOTES**
BREAKFAST			
SNACK			
LUNCH			
SNACK			
DINNER			
SNACK			

DATE:	SUPPLEMENTS:		
	FOOD & DRINKS	**SYMPTOMS**	**NOTES**
BREAKFAST			
SNACK			
LUNCH			
SNACK			
DINNER			
SNACK			

DATE:	SUPPLEMENTS:		
	FOOD & DRINKS	SYMPTOMS	NOTES
BREAKFAST			
SNACK			
LUNCH			
SNACK			
DINNER			
SNACK			

DATE:	SUPPLEMENTS:		
	FOOD & DRINKS	SYMPTOMS	NOTES
BREAKFAST			
SNACK			
LUNCH			
SNACK			
DINNER			
SNACK			

DATE:	SUPPLEMENTS:		
	FOOD & DRINKS	**SYMPTOMS**	**NOTES**
BREAKFAST			
SNACK			
LUNCH			
SNACK			
DINNER			
SNACK			

DATE:	SUPPLEMENTS:		
	FOOD & DRINKS	**SYMPTOMS**	**NOTES**
BREAKFAST			
SNACK			
LUNCH			
SNACK			
DINNER			
SNACK			

DATE:	SUPPLEMENTS:		
	FOOD & DRINKS	**SYMPTOMS**	**NOTES**
BREAKFAST			
SNACK			
LUNCH			
SNACK			
DINNER			
SNACK			

DATE:	SUPPLEMENTS:		
	FOOD & DRINKS	**SYMPTOMS**	**NOTES**
BREAKFAST			
SNACK			
LUNCH			
SNACK			
DINNER			
SNACK			

DATE:	SUPPLEMENTS:		
	FOOD & DRINKS	**SYMPTOMS**	**NOTES**
BREAKFAST			
SNACK			
LUNCH			
SNACK			
DINNER			
SNACK			

DATE:	SUPPLEMENTS:		
	FOOD & DRINKS	**SYMPTOMS**	**NOTES**
BREAKFAST			
SNACK			
LUNCH			
SNACK			
DINNER			
SNACK			

DATE:	SUPPLEMENTS:		
	FOOD & DRINKS	SYMPTOMS	NOTES
BREAKFAST			
SNACK			
LUNCH			
SNACK			
DINNER			
SNACK			

DATE:	SUPPLEMENTS:		
	FOOD & DRINKS	SYMPTOMS	NOTES
BREAKFAST			
SNACK			
LUNCH			
SNACK			
DINNER			
SNACK			

DATE:	SUPPLEMENTS:		
	FOOD & DRINKS	SYMPTOMS	NOTES
BREAKFAST			
SNACK			
LUNCH			
SNACK			
DINNER			
SNACK			

DATE:	SUPPLEMENTS:		
	FOOD & DRINKS	SYMPTOMS	NOTES
BREAKFAST			
SNACK			
LUNCH			
SNACK			
DINNER			
SNACK			

DATE:	SUPPLEMENTS:		
	FOOD & DRINKS	**SYMPTOMS**	**NOTES**
BREAKFAST			
SNACK			
LUNCH			
SNACK			
DINNER			
SNACK			

DATE:	SUPPLEMENTS:		
	FOOD & DRINKS	**SYMPTOMS**	**NOTES**
BREAKFAST			
SNACK			
LUNCH			
SNACK			
DINNER			
SNACK			

DATE:	SUPPLEMENTS:		
	FOOD & DRINKS	**SYMPTOMS**	**NOTES**
BREAKFAST			
SNACK			
LUNCH			
SNACK			
DINNER			
SNACK			

DATE:	SUPPLEMENTS:		
	FOOD & DRINKS	**SYMPTOMS**	**NOTES**
BREAKFAST			
SNACK			
LUNCH			
SNACK			
DINNER			
SNACK			

DATE:	SUPPLEMENTS:		
	FOOD & DRINKS	**SYMPTOMS**	**NOTES**
BREAKFAST			
SNACK			
LUNCH			
SNACK			
DINNER			
SNACK			

DATE:	SUPPLEMENTS:		
	FOOD & DRINKS	**SYMPTOMS**	**NOTES**
BREAKFAST			
SNACK			
LUNCH			
SNACK			
DINNER			
SNACK			

DATE:		SUPPLEMENTS:	
	FOOD & DRINKS	**SYMPTOMS**	**NOTES**
BREAKFAST			
SNACK			
LUNCH			
SNACK			
DINNER			
SNACK			

DATE:		SUPPLEMENTS:	
	FOOD & DRINKS	**SYMPTOMS**	**NOTES**
BREAKFAST			
SNACK			
LUNCH			
SNACK			
DINNER			
SNACK			

DATE:		SUPPLEMENTS:	
	FOOD & DRINKS	**SYMPTOMS**	**NOTES**
BREAKFAST			
SNACK			
LUNCH			
SNACK			
DINNER			
SNACK			

DATE:		SUPPLEMENTS:	
	FOOD & DRINKS	**SYMPTOMS**	**NOTES**
BREAKFAST			
SNACK			
LUNCH			
SNACK			
DINNER			
SNACK			

DATE:	SUPPLEMENTS:		
	FOOD & DRINKS	SYMPTOMS	NOTES
BREAKFAST			
SNACK			
LUNCH			
SNACK			
DINNER			
SNACK			

DATE:	SUPPLEMENTS:		
	FOOD & DRINKS	SYMPTOMS	NOTES
BREAKFAST			
SNACK			
LUNCH			
SNACK			
DINNER			
SNACK			

DATE:	SUPPLEMENTS:		
	FOOD & DRINKS	**SYMPTOMS**	**NOTES**
BREAKFAST			
SNACK			
LUNCH			
SNACK			
DINNER			
SNACK			

DATE:	SUPPLEMENTS:		
	FOOD & DRINKS	**SYMPTOMS**	**NOTES**
BREAKFAST			
SNACK			
LUNCH			
SNACK			
DINNER			
SNACK			

DATE:	SUPPLEMENTS:		
	FOOD & DRINKS	SYMPTOMS	NOTES
BREAKFAST			
SNACK			
LUNCH			
SNACK			
DINNER			
SNACK			

DATE:	SUPPLEMENTS:		
	FOOD & DRINKS	SYMPTOMS	NOTES
BREAKFAST			
SNACK			
LUNCH			
SNACK			
DINNER			
SNACK			

DATE:	SUPPLEMENTS:		
	FOOD & DRINKS	SYMPTOMS	NOTES
BREAKFAST			
SNACK			
LUNCH			
SNACK			
DINNER			
SNACK			

DATE:	SUPPLEMENTS:		
	FOOD & DRINKS	SYMPTOMS	NOTES
BREAKFAST			
SNACK			
LUNCH			
SNACK			
DINNER			
SNACK			

DATE:		SUPPLEMENTS:	
	FOOD & DRINKS	**SYMPTOMS**	**NOTES**
BREAKFAST			
SNACK			
LUNCH			
SNACK			
DINNER			
SNACK			

DATE:		SUPPLEMENTS:	
	FOOD & DRINKS	**SYMPTOMS**	**NOTES**
BREAKFAST			
SNACK			
LUNCH			
SNACK			
DINNER			
SNACK			

DATE:	SUPPLEMENTS:		
	FOOD & DRINKS	SYMPTOMS	NOTES
BREAKFAST			
SNACK			
LUNCH			
SNACK			
DINNER			
SNACK			

DATE:	SUPPLEMENTS:		
	FOOD & DRINKS	SYMPTOMS	NOTES
BREAKFAST			
SNACK			
LUNCH			
SNACK			
DINNER			
SNACK			

DATE:	SUPPLEMENTS:		
	FOOD & DRINKS	**SYMPTOMS**	**NOTES**
BREAKFAST			
SNACK			
LUNCH			
SNACK			
DINNER			
SNACK			

DATE:	SUPPLEMENTS:		
	FOOD & DRINKS	**SYMPTOMS**	**NOTES**
BREAKFAST			
SNACK			
LUNCH			
SNACK			
DINNER			
SNACK			

DATE:	SUPPLEMENTS:		
	FOOD & DRINKS	SYMPTOMS	NOTES
BREAKFAST			
SNACK			
LUNCH			
SNACK			
DINNER			
SNACK			

DATE:	SUPPLEMENTS:		
	FOOD & DRINKS	SYMPTOMS	NOTES
BREAKFAST			
SNACK			
LUNCH			
SNACK			
DINNER			
SNACK			

DATE:	SUPPLEMENTS:		
	FOOD & DRINKS	**SYMPTOMS**	**NOTES**
BREAKFAST			
SNACK			
LUNCH			
SNACK			
DINNER			
SNACK			

DATE:	SUPPLEMENTS:		
	FOOD & DRINKS	**SYMPTOMS**	**NOTES**
BREAKFAST			
SNACK			
LUNCH			
SNACK			
DINNER			
SNACK			

DATE:	SUPPLEMENTS:		
	FOOD & DRINKS	**SYMPTOMS**	**NOTES**
BREAKFAST			
SNACK			
LUNCH			
SNACK			
DINNER			
SNACK			

DATE:	SUPPLEMENTS:		
	FOOD & DRINKS	**SYMPTOMS**	**NOTES**
BREAKFAST			
SNACK			
LUNCH			
SNACK			
DINNER			
SNACK			

DATE:		SUPPLEMENTS:	
	FOOD & DRINKS	**SYMPTOMS**	**NOTES**
BREAKFAST			
SNACK			
LUNCH			
SNACK			
DINNER			
SNACK			

DATE:		SUPPLEMENTS:	
	FOOD & DRINKS	**SYMPTOMS**	**NOTES**
BREAKFAST			
SNACK			
LUNCH			
SNACK			
DINNER			
SNACK			

DATE:	SUPPLEMENTS:		
	FOOD & DRINKS	**SYMPTOMS**	**NOTES**
BREAKFAST			
SNACK			
LUNCH			
SNACK			
DINNER			
SNACK			

DATE:	SUPPLEMENTS:		
	FOOD & DRINKS	**SYMPTOMS**	**NOTES**
BREAKFAST			
SNACK			
LUNCH			
SNACK			
DINNER			
SNACK			

DATE:	SUPPLEMENTS:		
	FOOD & DRINKS	SYMPTOMS	NOTES
BREAKFAST			
SNACK			
LUNCH			
SNACK			
DINNER			
SNACK			

DATE:	SUPPLEMENTS:		
	FOOD & DRINKS	SYMPTOMS	NOTES
BREAKFAST			
SNACK			
LUNCH			
SNACK			
DINNER			
SNACK			

DATE:	SUPPLEMENTS:		
	FOOD & DRINKS	SYMPTOMS	NOTES
BREAKFAST			
SNACK			
LUNCH			
SNACK			
DINNER			
SNACK			

DATE:	SUPPLEMENTS:		
	FOOD & DRINKS	SYMPTOMS	NOTES
BREAKFAST			
SNACK			
LUNCH			
SNACK			
DINNER			
SNACK			

DATE:	SUPPLEMENTS:		
	FOOD & DRINKS	**SYMPTOMS**	**NOTES**
BREAKFAST			
SNACK			
LUNCH			
SNACK			
DINNER			
SNACK			

DATE:	SUPPLEMENTS:		
	FOOD & DRINKS	**SYMPTOMS**	**NOTES**
BREAKFAST			
SNACK			
LUNCH			
SNACK			
DINNER			
SNACK			

DATE:	SUPPLEMENTS:		
	FOOD & DRINKS	**SYMPTOMS**	**NOTES**
BREAKFAST			
SNACK			
LUNCH			
SNACK			
DINNER			
SNACK			

DATE:	SUPPLEMENTS:		
	FOOD & DRINKS	**SYMPTOMS**	**NOTES**
BREAKFAST			
SNACK			
LUNCH			
SNACK			
DINNER			
SNACK			

DATE:	SUPPLEMENTS:		
	FOOD & DRINKS	SYMPTOMS	NOTES
BREAKFAST			
SNACK			
LUNCH			
SNACK			
DINNER			
SNACK			

DATE:	SUPPLEMENTS:		
	FOOD & DRINKS	SYMPTOMS	NOTES
BREAKFAST			
SNACK			
LUNCH			
SNACK			
DINNER			
SNACK			

DATE:	SUPPLEMENTS:		
	FOOD & DRINKS	SYMPTOMS	NOTES
BREAKFAST			
SNACK			
LUNCH			
SNACK			
DINNER			
SNACK			

DATE:	SUPPLEMENTS:		
	FOOD & DRINKS	SYMPTOMS	NOTES
BREAKFAST			
SNACK			
LUNCH			
SNACK			
DINNER			
SNACK			

Notes

Notes

Notes

Notes

Tealous Books

Available from Amazon.com and other online stores.

Made in the USA
Las Vegas, NV
24 September 2021

30902629R00066